Legends of Leigh

LEGENDS OF LEIGH

SHEILA PITT-STANLEY

IAN HENRY PUBLICATIONS

First published 1989
New edition 1996

© Sheila E Pitt-Stanley, 1989, 1996

Pitt-Stanley, Sheila E
    Legends of Leigh
    1. Essex. Leigh-on-Sea, history
    I. Title
    942.6'795
    ISBN 0-86025-476-3

Most of the photographs are from the author's own collection,
but acknowledgement is made to
Ralph Pitt-Stanley, Alan J Ladget (for original glass plates), A J Walters,
Captain A Marriott, Max Fenning for `Doom Pond,, Chris Izod, and,
for `Lapwater Hall', Tony Pitt-Stanley.

Front cover: Billet Wharf. Tom Bell in centre of bench.

Printed by
Watkiss Studios, Ltd.
Holme Court, Biggleswade, Bedfordshire SG18 9ST
for
Ian Henry Publications, Ltd.
20 Park Drive, Romford, Essex RM1 4LH
01708 749119

I dedicate this book to my sons, Ralph, Tony and John,
and Douglas,
to my grandchildren,
Adam, Gavin, Donna, Hannah, Michaela and Ralph from New Zealand,
and to my friend Kim de Neumann
without whom publication would not have been possible.

Sheila Pitt-Stanley
President of the Leigh Society
Leigh, May, 1996

INTRODUCTION

On the north bank of the Thames, thirty miles east of London, stands the old fishing village of Leigh. Steeped in a wealth of history and legends of bygone days, tales have been handed down the corridors of time through generations of Leighmen and kept alive.

These stories have always fascinated me. When other children were enjoying Hans Andersen and Grimms' fairy tales, I was busy absorbing our local legends from my own family and any Leighman who had a tale to tell. Many I heard from `Hattie' Webster and Harry Thorp, the undertaker, both of them respected and encouraged my love of Leigh's history. When they, in their turn, were called to rest both entrusted me with their knowledge and their archives, knowing them to be in safe hands.

One particular fisherman I often called on after school was Tom Green of Billet Cottage, Billet Lane. Sometimes I found him on Billet Wharf and sometimes at his home. His tales enthralled me. Many of them he repeated over and over again, but I accepted them and listened as if it was the first telling, so anxious was I to know all he could recall.

As I grew older I began to suspect that some of his stories, such as the Sea Witch and the smuggling escapades, were too unrealistic to be true. And you may imagine my delight when, over the years, research proved most of them to be founded on fact.

I have always been intensely proud that my ancestors were part of Leigh's history. My maiden name was Brush and my grandfather, John Brush, came to Leigh from Surrey, via Leytonstone and Hadleigh, around the turn of the century. He purchased Leigh Park Brickfield and, as a master builder, contributed greatly to the development of the town. Old Town people, however, regarded him as a foreigner.

My mother's family goes back to Tudor times, coming from Tylty Grange, Essex, in about 1540. A name appears in the church

Tom Green

1

register for a baptism about that time, spelt Medley, and through the register over the centuries it recurs - with spelling variations according to the whim or pronunciation of the incumbent. Few Leighmen of those days could read or write and so the actual spelling was left to the rector's discretion.

It seems that the family either lacked imagination or, like myself, had a strong loyalty to tradition, because for many years the male line continues at regular intervals as either, for instance, William, Stephen, Thomas or George Meddle, until about 1846, when a birth was registered as Stephen Madle. About 1867 this Stephen married Matilda Smith, the name then being spelled Meddle.

Sir William Addison in *Essex Worthies* confirms the Tylty link saying, `The Marchioness of Dorset obtained from the Abbot of Tylty a lease for 60 years of the Grange and Manor of Tylty'. This lease was confirmed and allowed in 1538. Before she wed the Marquis, Lady Dorset had been the wife of William Meddle of Whitnash, Warwickshire, and she was succeeded at Tylty by her son, George Medley. This marriage was apparently not approved by Henry VIII, her uncle, who eventually annulled it to force her to marry Dorset.

In 1597 a Catharine and Thomas Meddle lived on the same pasture in the southwest corner of Billet Lane where my mother was born on 29th September, 1900, living there until her death on 6th January, 1982. When Catharine and Thomas lived there Leigh was just a clearing in the forest. The setting was once described by a much loved Leighman, Canon Robert S King (born 1862, died 1950) who said,

LEIGH - just an old world fishing village, dating back a thousand years and more, nestling at the foot of a steep hill, timbered in bygone days, almost to the water's edge,   the home of generations of hardy fisher-folk, and others who went down to the sea in ships, and after toilsome years, came back to the old place for a few years of quiet life, and then to their long rest under the shadow of the old church atop the hill.

The ebb and flow of the tide was all they had or needed to mark the passage of time.

Yes, this was the Leigh of the past. Its very name is a Saxon word *Legra* meaning the pasture or the place. And the church on the hill, St Clement's, with its 80 foot tower of Kentish ragstone, like a clenched fist forming a silhouette on the skyline, a guide to generations of returning Leigh seamen. The list of Rectors dates from 1248, but there is evidence of an earlier church on the same site.

Archæological discoveries verify our earliest history. In 1926 two hoards of Bronze Age weapons, dating from between 1000 and 750 BC, were found on the bank of Prittle Brook, near Kingswood Chase; Roman coins and pottery were found in my grandfather's brickfield to the west. In 1892 a skeleton was found in West Street with a bag of Saxon coins beneath its neck: the coins were given to Colchester Museum by H W King.

However, the earliest written record of Leigh is 1086, an entry in the *Domesday Book*. We know that it was a port of considerable importance and appears to have been the only town between Harwich and Gravesend. Certainly Plantagenet and Lancastrian kings and nobility embarked here for foreign travel. Its sheltered position inside the estuary made it most suitable. During the fourteenth century Leigh grew in importance and prosperity, but was in sad decline by the middle of the eighteenth century.

So many of the tales I learned as a child are also known to many Leigh people and have been passed from generation to generation. I am indeed grateful to my mother for making me a part of Leigh's proud heritage.

It was John Ruskin who summarised the feelings of those of us who love our historic past and I introduce the book with his words -

Watch this old town with anxious care, Guard it as best you may and at any cost from every influence of dilapidation.

Count its stones as you would jewels in a crown,

Set watches about it as if at the gates of a besieged city keeping the enemy at bay,

Bind it together with iron where it loosens,

Stay it with timber where it declines, and do this tenderly, reverently and continually and many generations yet to be born and live beneath its shadow will be grateful.

Sheila E Pitt-Stanley
Leigh
May, 1996

Leigh town from the marsh

3

LAPWATER HALL

Until November, 1947, Lapwater Hall stood in its own grounds on the London Road, between Burnham Road and Hadleigh Road, facing what is now the Black Rose Restaurant. It was an imposing red-brick house, well back from the road, approached from a curved gravel drive.

The main building was a double-fronted house with a magnificent pillared front door, embellished with a wonderful door knocker. The second wing, added in 1844 by Edmund Lampril, included a ballroom running from back to front, two kitchens and various servants' bedrooms.

Its original name was Leigh Park House and the story begins in 1750.

At that time the house was untenanted and practically a ruin. In about December that year news came to Leigh, via Rochford, that the solicitor had sold to a

stranger from London - a Mr Gilbert Craddock. A master builder had been engaged to re-build and there would be plenty of jobs for the locals. However, it was not until late January, 1751, when Essex roads lay deep in mud, that anything further happened.

Amos Tricker lived and had always lived between the turnpike at Eastwood Road and Leigh Park House, being employed by the owners of Leigh Park Farm as a general labourer. I am sure his descendants, who live in Highfield Gardens, Westcliff, will forgive my saying that he was a typical farm hand of his day, who could neither read nor write.

That January morning he was there, cutting back hedges opposite the house, when he heard a horseman coming at a gallop and, when a mud-splashed stranger reined up before him and asked if this was Leigh Park House, Amos could only stare

The Turnpike, Eastwood Road

4

at the questioner's fine brown mare with her snake-like head and no ears!

Mr Craddock was used to this reaction and, when he saw Amos nodding vacantly, he tossed a small coin, jumped his horse neatly over the fence and inspected the property. Later, with a nod at the still-gaping farmhand, he rode off in the direction of Eastwood and, presumably on to Rochford.

In early February work began. Leigh men were indeed employed as bricklayers, carpenters and labourers and their small daily wage was supplemented by three pots of ale a day. Amos was employed as a beer carrier, pushing a handcart, several times a day, up the white cockleshell path known then (and now) as Leigh Park Road and across the fields - Tikle and Ducksmead - carrying the workmen's ale and stock for Mr Craddock's cellar.

Craddock himself made several trips to Leigh and, on those occasions, stayed at the Smack, where he stabled his horse, Brown Meg.

It was obvious that he was anxious to take up residence as soon as possible; he was always dissatisfied with the slow progress the workmen were making and, in any event, the Leigh men regarded him, along with anyone else of his standing, as a 'furriner' and with suspicion and distrust.

He did make some friends, however; one evening he called at the Rectory to make some arrangements for his wedding the first week in June. He was told that the Rector was down the hill dining with Henry Thompson at Eden Lodge. He was shown on to the terrace, where Mr Thompson and the Reverend Roger Price were taking their port. They instantly saw in him a gentleman of education and breeding and found him a skilled and worthy opponent in the subtle man uvres of chess. And so it subsequently became a regular thing for him to dine either at the Rectory or Eden Lodge when in Leigh. He hoped to move in to Leigh Park House in early May, but when he arrived at the site in March and found the roof still untiled, he was not very pleased. The men, how-ever, were glad to see him on that particular day, because custom decreed that when the last beam of the building was placed in position, the workmen would cheer the owner and receive a round of ale to wish good luck to the house.

Mr Craddock stood below and watched the operation with interest, but when the men downed tools and gathered around him with grins of anticipation, he did not understand the custom nor did the occasion delight him. When his apparent ignorance of the custom could only be met with a frank demand for beer, he turned on them with rage and said: "Beer, you boozy scabs! Don't I pay you for it every minute of the time you rob me of... and more. If drink you must have, go to the pond and lap water as better dogs do every day. Lap water, you saucy hounds!"

And turning to the master builder he demanded that he taught them the respect due to a gentleman and to exhort them to double their efforts as he intended to move in in four weeks or every one of them would be working for half pay.

The men brooded on this affront all day, repeating over and over again Craddock's threats and grumbling at his meanness until it occurred to them that the only way to get even with this `furriner' was to turn his words back on him. He had had the audacity to tell honest Leighmen to `lap water' from a horse pond. They were words he would regret saying - they would see to it that they hit back at him all the days of his life for that was what they would dub his fine house: Lapwater Hall.

For the rest of that day they passed the word back and forth amongst themselves with confident laughter: they had evened the score. Leigh had had the last word. That night the new name was spoken in every ale house within five miles and by the time the house was completed it was firmly in the minds of one and all.

When the Rector, on behalf of his absent friend, installed Mrs Fiddler as housekeeper and Nan Tricker as parlour-maid, Mrs Fiddler had to constantly remind Nan tt remember to use only the old name in the master's hearing.

It was about a week before the May Fair that Gilbert Craddock did move in. He spent most of that first afternoon looking around the farm and the brickfields and, after an early dinner, walked down to the Smack to collect Meg. He stopped at Eden Lodge and sat for a while on the terrace with Henry Thompson and his son-in-law and daughter, William and Elizabeth Little. It was from Elizabeth that the greater part of this story was obtained.

She said that Gilbert was very happy that night; everything about his house and farm pleased him and it seemed to be the fulfilment of a dream. Final arrangements were being made for the wedding and the bride, Lady Eleanor, was to be their guest and married from Eden Lodge.

Gilbert Craddock continued his journey to the Smack and, as he entered the noisy bar, suddenly all conversation ceased but for the voice of one big, red-headed fisher-man, Sam Gilson, who got to his feet and continued to address his mates, "Shet up! Why should I shet up? He ain't no gentleman wot tells his fellow men to lap water... he ain't even no man. Lapwater Hall!" he laughed right in Craddock's face.

Craddock grabbed his big red ear and sent him crashing against the panelled wall. Gilson rushed back at him, but cowered under a hail of lashes from Craddock's riding whip. A whack on the table made the pots jump and Craddock turned on his heel and walked out. He rode up the hill like a demon from hell and, as he turned into his own stable yard, he saw a wagon delivering crockery and Nan emerging from the back door with a mug of ale in her hand.

"Oh, sir, 'tis for the wagoner," she explained. "He came so late and couldn't find Leigh Park House, but came here guessing it must be Lapwater -"

"Go on, damn ye, say it. Lapwater Hall. They shan't give my house that name for nothing," and he grabbed the mug and flung it across the yard. "By God, if anyone drinks ought but water here, I'll take it back with a carving knife." He strode through the conservatory into the hall to turn the key in the cellar door and put it in his pocket. From then on he always carried it with him.

In the weeks that followed Mr Craddock went off on trips that lasted two or three days at a time. "Gawn-a-courtin', I

Leigh Park House 'Lapwater Hall'. Painting by Tony Pitt-Stanley

7

shouldn't wonder, poor gentleman," Mrs Fiddler would tell Nan.

He was away about the third week in May and somewhere nearby a dog howled. "It's abaying death," said Nan, and the candle too gave the sign of death rising in a straight column of smoke.

Suddenly the eerie silence was broken. "'Tis the master," said Nan. "It sounds as if the mare's gone lame."

Moments later the door was kicked open and there, indeed, stood the master, mud-splashed and blood streaming from his right sleeve. He emptied the water jug at one pull and, taking off his jacket, he ordered the women to bind his arm, then to dowse the lights and bar the door behind him and answer the door to no one.

They heard him shut the door and walk to the London Road and then pass around the back. For a while all was quiet and then the road suddenly seemed alive with horsemen, some shouting: "Look, there's the house, perhaps we can get some fresh horses. I think we've lost him."

Then there came a loud knocking and an authoritative voice commanded, "Open the door in the King's name!" The knocking continued and a voice from the back called, "He's, here, sir. The mare's steaming in the stable." Then came the sound of something heavy crashing on the door and, on the third blow, the doorknocker was smashed. The fourth forced the door open and the house was searched from top to bottom.

The officer in charge told Mrs Fiddler that the felon they sought was Cutter Lynch, the highwayman. They had heard that he planned to retire from the road and that night they had had the luck to flush him near Shenfield. Shots had been exchanged and Cutter Lynch was wounded in his arm. One of the Bow Street Runners had fallen dead in his saddle, but they had chased the highwayman through Ingrave, Horndon, Laindon and Pitsea. Somehow his mare had gone lame or they would never have kept within hailing distance of Brown Meg. He knew every dyke and fence at Benfleet and had foxed them so completely that, by the time they reached Castle Hill, he was far ahead, walking his horse up the next hill in the moonlight towards the London Road.

When dawn broke they resumed their search of the grounds and at around six they found Meg, shivering and whinnying on the edge of the pond and, floating near the reeds, was an upturned tricorn hat and inside was a black mask and a pair of wax horse ears that clipped to the headstall used when Mr Gilbert Craddock was Cutter Lynch!

Rakes and grommets were brought and the pond dragged; from a culvert at the far end they brought up Gilbert Craddock's body. They assumed that he had hidden among the reeds, hanging on to the bank until, possibly, loss of blood had induced faintness and he had drowned. Leighmen gathering later in the day said they thought it a proper end for a `furriner' who told Leighmen to drink from the very same pond when he owed them ale.

Three days later, on 21st May, he was interred in St Clement's churchyard and, later at Eden Lodge, Lady Eleanor told his friends that he had promised to give up the road when she agreed to marry him. This was to have been his last ride. They had planned to live quietly as squire and lady.

"We could have been so happy here," she ended wistfully.

That should have been the end of the story - but it wasn't.

In June Nan Tricker married Tim Livermore of Belfairs, the party afterwards being held in the upper rooms of the Billet. Amos, feeling merry from the large quantities of ale he had consumed, got to thinking of all the fine wines and brandies he had carried over to Lapwater Hall and, although the house stood locked and shuttered, he knew where the keys were. He convinced himself that, since Craddock was dead, no one had more right to the booty than he had. After all, hadn't he carried every bottle and barrel of it?

So he made his way to the house, entering like the master through the front door into the dark hall, down six cellar steps. He turned to the left, but got no further, for there, facing him, in an arched recess, stood Gilbert Craddock, mug in hand and actually offering him a drink. Amos turned and fled. He, who had been the first man in Leigh to see Gilbert Craddock, was now the first to see his ghost! Leighmen then decided that Craddock was obliged to remain earthbound, haunting Lapwater Hall, until someone accepted his hospitality - thus redeeming the insult he had inflicted on them.

As for the house, it remained in Lady Eleanor's possession. She made regular visits to Leigh, staying either there or at Eden Lodge. Eventually, to please her family, she made a marriage of social convenience, which carried a title. But Lapwater Hall remained her own private

shrine to the memory of her one love.

Upon her death the house passed to a nephew, Benjamin Farrand, and, on 28th August, 1841, was conveyed to Edmund Lampril, by indenture. He resided there for 41 years, 21 as tenant and 20 as proprietor, in 1844 enlarging the house with a new wing. He died in 1862 and, after his widow's death in 1864 the house was again sold.

Just over a hundred years after Gilbert and Eleanor's tragedy the Hall was again redecorated and prepared for a newly-married couple. The bride was Ann Turpin (no relation to the notorious highwayman, Dick), her father being a merchant, William Turpin of Bishopsgate, London. The bridegroom was Anthony Blackborne of 35 Audley Street, Grosvenor Square, who came from Great Gusted Hall, Rochford.

I like to think that they experienced all the happiness that was denied to Gilbert and Eleanor.

One of the keys to Lapwater Hall

THE STRAND

The Strand is the oldest existing wharf in Leigh today. What tales this ancient quay could tell! Even on that sad day in 1940 when Southend Corporation began their scandalous demolition of Leigh's age-old dwellings it produced three priceless relics from its distant past, confirming its connection with former occupants - the Masters of Trinity House.

For, beneath no less than nine layers of wallpaper, oak panelling was revealed, together with the nickel-plated butterfly door hinges dating back to Tudor times. In January, 1533, Strand Wharf was part of the dowry of Anne Boleyn on her marriage to Henry VIII and, from about 1615, was known to have been occupied by Richard Chester, a Master of Trinity House. Behind the Tudor panelling, beneath nine layers of wallpaper, `Neb' Osborne found secreted

The panelling in Richard Chester's house

three prayer books bound in white hide, hand-written on vellum: the prayers of Trinity House dated 1616.

In July, 1620, religious folk from all over Essex converged upon Leigh to join the *Mayflower*, moored off the Strand. She had commenced her voyage from Wapping Old Stairs and had docked at Leigh to revittle and receive the Essex pilgrims. The *Mayflower* was part-owned by John Vassal of Cockethurst Farm, Eastwood.

Leigh folk, however, were reluctant to join the pilgrims to the New World; they questioned the wisdom of such a dangerous journey. They said the *Mayflower* was too

The *Mayflower* off Leigh, July, 1620
Painted by Vic Ellis
[by kind permission of Bernard C Willder]

Cockett House; the home of John Vassell, part owner of the *Mayflower*

11

small for all these passengers, plus those due to embark at Plymouth. They said she was old and unseaworthy and would never reach her destination.

How wrong they were!

In 1255 Leigh Strand had been the scene of a royal intrigue. Lodged at the Crown were a young couple obviously very much in love, waiting for a ship to carry them to France. Leigh folk were impressed by their elegance and their rich fur trimmed clothes and how surprised they would have been had they known that the beautiful girl was none other than Princess Beatrice, daughter of King Henry III, who was attempting to elope with Ralph de Binley, the man of her choice. Meanwhile, in London, her father was negotiating with Spanish diplomats the details of her marriage alliance with Alfonse, Lord of Castille.

When at last the awaited ship docked and was ready to depart the innkeeper lit their path towards the steps on the south side of the quay, when suddenly from the shadows a foreign merchant challenged them and, in a frenzied attempt to stop their departure, he drew a knife. Ralph instinctively fought to save his princess and, in the struggle that ensued, the merchant fell on his own dagger and was instantly killed.

The innkeeper urged them to get aboard as soon as possible and he undertook to dispose of the body, but the merchant, in the hope of a reward, had an hour since sent word to the Bailiff of Hadleigh Castle for guards to apprehend the couple. The Princess was arrested and taken back to London and her father, while Ralph was brought to trial at Chelmsford and sentenced to death.

Beatrice pleaded with her father to spare her lover, while promising to marry whosoever the King should dictate. She travelled to Chelmsford and presented the Royal Pardon and Ralph was taken back to Leigh to be deported and exiled from England forever. The princess travelled with him to the port.

It is said that the Princess stood on the Strand Steps watching until the ship was lost to her sight at the mouth of the Thames and only then could the innkeeper's wife persuade the grief-stricken girl to return to the warmth of the inn.

About a year later the princess returned to Leigh at her father's wish to embark for France to marry John of Brittany. It is improbable that she and her lover ever met again.

Tom Green told a strange tale about a ship from Calais that moored on the Strand just before daybreak one morning in late summer about 1397. A lead coffin was unloaded and lay on the Strand all day. Drawn by curiosity and superstitious fear, Leigh folk gathered to see it at first hand and speculate on its contents. Questions directed at the crew revealed little beyond the fact that the deceased was of blood royal and an uncle of King Richard.

All morning the hot sun beat down on the mysterious object and, at midday, Leighmen, moved by loyalty and respect for the dead, carried the coffin into a house on the Strand, placing it on a wide mantelshelf inside. There it remained until shortly before midnight, when a chariot was sent from Hadleigh Castle to collect this macabre cargo.

I questioned my great-grandfather, Mark, about this story and he confirmed it emphatically: his grandfather had told him, but he knew no more of the historic background than Tom Green did. This is possibly a remarkable example of handed-down lore, as Jean Froissart's *Chronicles*, in a long account of treason and plotting in 1397, recorded that Thomas of Woodstock, Duke of Gloucester and uncle of Richard II, had been strangled at Calais. His body had been embalmed, encased in lead and conveyed by sea to the Castle of Hadley upon Thames side and from there to his own church at Pleshey.

In 1406 Henry IV, endeavouring to avoid the plague then raging in London, crossed the Thames from Sheppey to Leigh. When he was only halfway across, His ship was attacked by French pirates; a great chase ensued and, had it not been for the skill and navigational prowess of his crew, the King would undoubtedly have been captured. As he set foot on the Strand, the King went down on his knees and, with his eyes firmly fixed on the church on the hill, he gave thanks to God for his safe delivery to Leigh. He was then persuaded to take refreshment at the Crown on the Strand before continuing his journey to Pleshey.

Historians Fox and Benton relate that in 1554 Frances, Marchioness of Dorset, daughter of Mary Tudor and Charles Brandon and mother of Lady Jane Grey, escaped from Leigh. She remained during the day in the house of a merchant, Joslin, and slept at the Crown Inn on the Strand by night. When the tide flowed at early dawn she escaped in a fast fishing boat belonging to George Medley, a son of her first marriage to William Medley of Tylty Grange, Essex.

Richard Chester's steps, 1615

13

ST CLEMENTS CHURCH

The Font

Prior to the restoration of the church the font was of modern and barbarous character. It was replaced by another of quasi-perpendicular design. This was removed in 1871 and a third substituted - a copy of the font in St Mary's, Prittlewell, the panels showing the Tudor rose and the Aragon pomegranate, thus deceiving one into thinking of it as early Tudor. This font was recently replaced with one from St Swithin's Church, Norwich, a church made redundant because of the depopulation of its parish: it is exactly contemporary with the oldest parts of St Clements. The font and cover are in memory of all the members of the Bundock family who have worshipped in St Clement's over the centuries. On each of the eight sides is a symbol in a quatrefoil, alternately sacred and family symbols, the former distinguished by the gilding of their quatrefoils. These symbols are a Byzantine Cross; a Lamb and a Flag for the Resurrection, signifying that we die with Christ in our Baptism and rise again to a newness of life, a theme well developed by St Paul; a Dove in flight, signifying the Holy Spirit; and an Anchor, for St Clement. On the wall above the font is a painting of John the Baptist baptising Jesus - now hidden by emulsion paint. The beautiful statue of the Madonna and Holy Child was given as a thanks offering for the recovery of the Holy Land from the Turks.

The Cutlass Stone

Facing the red brick Tudor porch stands the red brick Cutlass Stone, topped by an altar stone. Tradition tells us that the press-gang respectfully waited for services to end before pressing the young, able-bodied youth of Leigh and would pass the time by sharpening their cutlasses on the tomb of Mary Ellis, who died in 1609.

When the congregation heard the dreadful sound of sword upon stone they knew the press-gang had been unable to acquire the required quota of men from the waterside pubs and were outside the church. The sexton would watch from a slit window on the steps of the church tower and the young men inside would lift a flagstone in the floor of the church, descending twelve steps to the crypt and go west through a subterranean passage to the cellar of the Rectory which stood due south of what was then Leigh House. There they hid. When the service ended the congregation emerged - old women, young girls and men far too old to be of use to His Majesty's Navy. Much later, when the press-gang boats were seen to be well out in the estuary, towards the mouth of the Thames, the young men came out of hiding - no doubt thanking God and St Clement for their safe delivery from a fate worse than death. In 1875 the last surviving Leighman who had suffered this fate, Goldspring Thompson, died aged 97.

Over the years the tomb became obliterated through weather and misuse, but in May, 1794, when the inscription was still readable, a reporter from the *London Chronicle*, who happened to pass through the churchyard, was so amused by the inscription that he had it printed in his paper. From this source I found it on microfilm in Fleet Street and, in 1966, I asked the Rev John L Head to reinstate it

St Clement's Church

on a temporary white painted patch on top
of the tomb and, when I became President
of the Leigh Society, we made it a priority
project. With exhibitions and public
donations we were able to commission an
ecclesiastical mason to inscribe the epitaph
on a slab of Forest of Dean stone inserted
into the brickwork.

The epitaph reads

Here lies the body of Mary Ellis, daughter
of Thomas & Lydia Ellis of this parish. She
was a virgin of virtuous courage &
promising hope and died on the 3rd of
June 1609 aged 119.

Recently schoolchildren have said that
this is the tomb of a witch, but Mary Ellis
was a much loved and respected member

The cutlass stone

of the community, for which reason she
was given this place of honour in front of
the church door. When Leigh folk were sick
and could not afford doctors, she would
provide the herbal remedies, like salt bags
for earaches or goosefat for sore throats.
She was certainly no witch!

The Deal family

Through the door on the east side of the tower is a stone spiral staircase and it was here, one Sunday morning in a 19th century May, that the sexton, upon opening the church, heard a child crying pitifully behind the locked door. On his release the terrified boy, estimated to be about six years old, told how he had come to Leigh with travelling people to Leigh's annual May Fair.

In the villages visited by the fair people, being small and agile he was forced through church windows against his will in order to rob poor boxes. In St Clement's Church, however, the only accessible window was the west window in the tower.

He had climbed the ivy on the tower and dropped from the small window sill to the floor of the bell chamber. He had then descended the steps only to find the door bolted from the other side and he could not get into the church itself. On returning to the bell chamber he had found the sheer depth from the floor back to the window impossible to negotiate. All night he had tried in vain and, just before dawn's first light, the fair people had abandoned him lest they should be caught.

The sexton quite naturally questioned the boy's identity and, between tears and sobbing, the only name distinguishable was `Deal'. Whether it was Deal in Kent he had come from or whether that was his name they never really established, but `Churchie' Deal was brought up with a respectable Leigh family and his line exists here

`Churchie' Deal

prominently today. When `Churchie' died in 1913 it was estimated that he left a hundred descendants.

16

The interior of St Clement's in the eighteenth century

The Altar Window

The east window above the High Altar is painted in enamel and represents the Crucifixion with figures of the Blessed Virgin Mary, St Mary Magdalene and St John - also a Roman soldier and a white horse. This window has a twin in a Belgian cathedral, but the Flemish horse is black.

Three times Canon Walker King commissioned an artist from the National Portrait Gallery to paint or enamel our horse black to match, but he obviously had a mind of his own and prefers himself white, for on each occasion he rejected the enamel and returned to his own colour.

The whole style of this window is that of the later masters in the art. In 1870, the year of the great storm in the Thames Estuary, parts of the window were shattered and Canon Walker King, incumbent at the time, was responsible for the most unsuitable glass that replaced it. The top is such a complete contrast to the enamelled splendour of the original.

17

The church tower

Lady Olivia was a wonderful friend to Leigh and was probably Leigh's greatest benefactress. She sought to educate the children and established a Dame School in Hall Road (as it then was), now the Broadway. The northern end of the building was where the back of Woolworth's is now. Eventually in 1834 she built the School House, still standing today in 'mid-hill' facing 'The Gardens', which in those days were the lime kilns. The very first teacher was Dr Herschell and the school became known as Herschell School. Behind it is the house and garden Dr Herschell occupied and this piece of land runs from the school up to the edge of St

Lady Olivia Sparrow

Lady Olivia Sparrow

A window on the south side of the High Altar is dedicated to the Honourable Lady Olivia Sparrow, who was once Lady of the Manor. Her house was Leigh Hall, which was where the timberyard is now in the aptly named Leigh Hall Road. The Hall dated from 1561 and faced south with an overhanging upper storey and possessed fine, dark Spanish oak panelling.

Lady Sparrow's school, Midd Hill

Clement's churchyard. Herschell House is also still standing: for some years it was called Ivy Cottage, but in 1978 local restaurateur, Dennis Hill, bought the house and restored the original name.

Lady Olivia also recognised the need for increased water supplies and, in 1832, she had a well dug in the centre of the Strand. In 1836 she financed a second near Bell Wharf and another near Tiklehouse.

The window in the church was installed purely from respect and gratitude; she was not a member of the congregation, claiming to be 'low church'. It seems that this was

Leigh Hall manor house, the home of Lady Olivia

Herschel House

mainly because of a feud with Rev Robert Eden and she is not buried in the churchyard It was her wish to be buried with her family at Brampton, Huntingdon, and when she died, on 12th February, 1863, her wishes were carried out.

Unfortunately, her commemorative window, in the obscure position that it holds, is not noticed by many people, but it was taken from an original design exhibited at the Royal Academy in 1779 by Sir Joshua Reynolds. The panels show two figures, Faith and Hope. Usually one associates Faith, Hope and Charity together

The National Schools, built by the Revd. Robert Eden

Lady Sparrow's Well on the Strand. Richard Chester's house in background

as a threesome, so why was Charity omitted from the memorial of this lady, whose very life was based entirely on charitable deeds? One can only imagine that her coat of arms in the lower panel was intended to portray Lady Olivia herself as Charity.

It must be recorded that a latter day tribute was indeed paid to her. Because the education of children was so close to her heart her coat of arms - the double headed eagle - was chosen as the badge of Belfairs High School, built on land which was once hers. Credit for this gesture must be given to the late Councillor Bert Mussett.

Benton, the historian, once said, "She was a great benefactress and her name will long be remembered in Leigh." What a pity that only the minimum of recognition was allowed by her adversary, Robert Eden, and that in the most concealed part of the parish church, minus a memorial plate.

She was remembered as recently as 1978, when at a service of dedication a brass plate was fixed below her coat of arms, inscribed

This window is dedicated to the
memory of
LADY OLIVIA BERNARD
SPARROW

Lady of the Manor and benefactress of
Leigh who died on 12 February, 1863.
Plaque laid by 'The Leigh Society' in July,
1978.   Engraved by John Howson.

And so the insult was avenged by the
grateful people of Leigh.

As a fitting conclusion to this section
and a further possible epitaph to the great
lady, it is interesting to note that Olivia
Drive was named after her; Manchester
Drive after her daughter, the Duchess of
Manchester; Lord Robert's Avenue after her
husband or her son, who were both Lord
Roberts; and Leigh Hall Road where her
manor stood.

Vandalism

The *Gentleman's Magazine* for 1865 reports
a tragic tale of 19th century vandalism
written by eminent local historian and
conservationist, H W King, who says

My attention was first directed to the
spoliation in 1842 and on visiting the
church I found that two monumental
inscriptions in brass had been abstracted -
one in memory of the ancient family of
Salmon, dated 1472, and another for the
family of Bonner, dated 1580; that the
marble tablet in memory of Admiral
Nicholas Haddock had been totally
destroyed; that three memorial tablets and
brasses had been removed from the church;
and that other acts of vandalism had been
committed.

From correspondence in my possession
it seems that these memorials were absent
from the church for three or four years.
Repeated application was made to the Rev.
Eden for their restoration, but all know-
ledge of their existence was denied. Further
enquiries were made - at length it was
discovered that they were 'in a lumber
room at the rectory' or - as I am now, I
think, more correctly informed - 'concealed
in loft over the rectory stable'. Application
for their restitution was at once renewed
and at last, they were taken to the church
and placed on the floor of the vestry, when
they stood exposed to injury at least as late
as 1848 and, I think, until 1858.

In 1880 Mr King was apparently still
very anxious about this deplorable
situation. He had in his possession papers
relating to the Chesters of Leigh. With yet
another desperate attempt to put things
back in their rightful places, he wrote to
the Editor of the *Chelmsford Chronicle*
saying

Mr George Chester resided at Leigh, where
he died in 1649 aged fifty four. His and his
first wife's effigies have long done duty as
the portraiture of the gallant Welsh
commander, John Price, and his wife,
whose inscription plate of a much later
date, is inlaid beneath the figures on the
same slab. These effigies are curious from
the circumstances of being executed in
profile with averted faces. Although the
inscription plate has been abstracted and
that in the memory of Captain Price laid
down in its place. I feel confident that I
have correctly appropriated the effigies.

George Chester and his wife

We owe the misunderstanding of the relics of this naval worthy to his friendship with Admiral Sir Edward Whitaker of Leigh House, who was connected by marriage to Chester Moore, (then representative of the Chesters); both he and Sir Edward married daughters of Thomas Stevens. Other than this Captain Price had no connection with Leigh whatsoever. They, no doubt, gave the Captain his last resting place in their own family grave. His memorial on the north wall is almost adjoining the epitaph of the Whitakers causing, however, a striking anachronism between the costume of the effigies and the inscription, the costume is so obviously of an earlier date than the inscription.

The connection between the Moores and the Whitakers is confirmed by Philip Benton in his *History of the Rochford Hundred*. Thomas Stevens of Leigh, a surgeon, had three daughters; Elizabeth,

UNDERNEATH THIS STONE LYETH BURYED THE BODY OF RICHARD CHESTER OF THIS PARISH MARINER WHO WHILEST HE LIVED WAS ONE OF THE ELDER BROTHERS OF THE TRINITY HOUSE AND WAS MASTER OF THE SAID SOCIETY IN THE YERE OF OUR LORD 1615 HE LIVED IN MARRIAGE WITH ELIZABETH HIS WIFE ABOUT 9 YEERES BY WHOM HE HAD ISSUE 4 SONNS AND ONE DAUGHTER OF WHICH NUMBER ONLY GEORGE AND ROBERT CHESTER HIS SONNS AND ELIZABETH HIS DAUGHTER SURVIVED HIM   HE DECEASSED THE 5TH DAY OF APRILL 1632 AND HIS SAID TWO SONNS GEORGE & ROBERT PLACED THIS STONE HERE IN REMEMBRANCE OF THEIRE SAIDE DECEASSED FATHER

Richard and Elizabeth Chester

wife of Chester Moore, Esq.; Ann, wife of Sir Edward Whitaker; and Mary, wife of Captain Samuel Whitaker, his brother. What more proof can I offer than the testimonials of these two great historians?

Richard Chester, a wealthy mariner, came to Leigh in the late 1590s from Hartlepool, County Durham. He became a Master of Trinity House in 1615. George, his eldest son, was born in Leigh and so, subsequently, were the rest of his family, five in all, residing on The Strand. The male line died out in 1652. Obviously proud of the lineage, Chester was used as a Christian name by their distaff descendants down to the 18th century, through two changes of surname.

In 1632 Richard Chester died, George and his brother, Robert, being responsible for the brass effigy placed at the foot of the chancel steps, in memory of their parents. It is reasonable to assume that, in turn, George was similarly honoured.

In 1865 Mr King wrote to the *Gentleman's Magazine* stating that he had again sought after these memorials and was informed that nothing was known of them. On further investigation I found the man who had been a servant to the rector and was promoted to the office of sexton. From under the very eyes of the clergy and churchwardens and without attracting observation he conveyed three framed oaken panels with inscriptions and devices curiously illuminated in gold and colours and richly emblazoned with armorial bearings, in memory of a distinguished naval officer, Captain John Rogers; he

obliterated the inscriptions, defaced the arms and then cut and adapted it to a cupboard door: the fate of the others I cannot learn.

Now we know this to be true, because, not many years since, the oaken panels were found in a fisherman's cottage down the hill and in Bank House there are other church treasures. High above the fireplace is a large medallion of the Madonna and Child. There are also four stained glass windows far older than the house itself; one is the coat of arms of Lord Rich, Earl of Warwick, Lord of the Manor, who had the right of presentation of the living of Leigh church and others of the Rochford Hundred. The second window is a memorial to Richard III, who died in 1485 at Bosworth Field - he was married to Anne, daughter of the Earl of Warwick. The loveliest window is the Haddock coat of arms; the Haddocks who were the illustrious benefactors of Leigh for four hundred years. The fourth window is a representation of St Catherine, with a lance and wheel.

All clearly given and dedicated with reverence and respect to glorify and enhance the church, surely not to adorn the walls and windows of a private residence that stands in constant jeopardy from developers upon whose slightest whim the whole building could be totally destroyed and those beautiful objects lost forever.

Bank House

Bank House
on left;
Lady Sparrow's
School, 2nd left

The Cotgroves

The stained glass window depicting the Good Shepherd has made its beautiful contribution to the north wall of St Clement's Church since 20 June, 1887. It took the people of Leigh thirteen years to raise the money, in pennies, ha'pennies and farthings, but slowly but surely the funds were raised.

In all those years the fishermen never forgot or ceased to mourn William Cotgrove and his father, 'Judgement' Cotgrove, whose boat capsized in a squall off Woolwich one cold December day. It was not until the following month that their bodies were recovered off Rainham and, on 22 January, they were brought back by boat and the two coffins placed in the crowded church.

The brass plate underneath the window reads

This window was offered to the church in affectionate memory of W J Cotgrove, fisherman, who was drowned December 11th, 1874, in his 21st year.

But why no mention of 'Judgement', his father? The register of burials records two deaths and funeral bills confirm that on 22 January, 1875, two bodies were removed from the boat: Two coffins with best furniture, 12 bearers and 2 palls at the cost of £3.6.0d and fees for the grave 4/6d. William J (Judgement) Cotgrove was a deeply religious man. Only ten months before he and his friend Abraham 'Happy' Partridge had walked to Stone to be confirmed and now God had called him home to rest.

Surely he too deserved to be remembered.

27

The Haddocks

The Haddocks lived in the southeast corner of Workhouse Lane, now Billet Lane. This name derived from their house, The Old Billet, a seamen's billet (now misnamed The Crooked Billet) and the original name of the lane came from the workhouse the Haddocks built on the west side of the road.

Sir Richard Haddock, possibly the most famous of them all and well respected by his contemporaries, sold this house in 1707. Horatio Nelson remarked, referring to his prize money, "All of it honestly come by, as Old Haddock once said - 'Not a penny of it is dirty money'".

The Haddocks were, in fact, resident benefactors of Leigh for four hundred years. In 1672, at the Battle of Sole Bay, Richard was wounded in the foot and was almost the only surviving officer of the flagship the *Royal James*. On 3 July, 1675, Charles II knighted Admiral Haddock and also, as a mark of royal favour, the King took the satin cap from his own head and placed it on that of Sir Richard. The cap was long preserved in the family with an account of the circumstances of its acquisition pinned to it.

Sadly, there are no Haddocks left in Leigh, but on 11 August, 1969, the daughter of James Henry Haddock came to St Clements from Dallas, Texas, and the following year John Haddock came from Virginia. In 1971 Nelson Haddock came from Tasmania. All were anxious to re-establish the Haddock connection with Leigh and St Clement's and were delighted with the preservation of the history of their famous ancestors.

The Crooked Billet

The family can be traced back in Leigh from the time of Edward III in 1430 in the Harleian manuscripts (in the archives of Oxford University). From this source comes the letter dated 1694 from a Miss Isabella Critchley, daughter of Admiral Sir John Critchley, to Sir Richard Haddock.

Leigh, Wednesday night of 4th July 1694

Your good nature, Sir, hath drawne upon you the gossupin of a company of women. My sisters desire that we may drinke our punch with you tomorrow in the evening about six o'clocke, if it be not inconvenient to you.

I should have sent you today, but was prevented.

However Sir, it may yet be ajourned if you are Otherwise disposed.

The doctors are sending me to Tunbridge ere long. So that a warm foundation, before place drinking those cold waters will not be amiss for Sr.

Your obliged humble servant.

For Sir Richard Haddock, these.

Isabella Critchley

He was a fine man and very wealthy, could she have had designs on him, one wonders?

On the wall of the Chapel of Resurrection in Leigh church is a brass erected to the memory of their predecessors, who for a long period carried on the work of their Guild at the port of Leigh. The 15th century a Guild of Pilots was formed at Leigh, closely associated with a similar organisation at Deptford. Leigh provided pilots for inward vessels and Deptford for the outward bound. These Guilds were united by Henry VIII and from then on the Brotherhood was known as the Fraternity of the Most Glorious and Indivisible Trinity and of St Clement.

In 1514 the Society of Brethren, as they were called, were incorporated by Royal Charter of Henry VIII and its privileges were confirmed and extended by subsequent charters, chiefly by that of James II in 1685. The Merchant Shipping Act, 1854, laid on Trinity House the duty of removing dangerous wrecks. Their motto is 'Trinitas in Unitate'.

The object of the fraternity was to preserve the lives of seamen on land and sea, to appoint pilots, place buoys and sea marks, and to grant licences to poor seamen not free of the City to row on the Thames for their support in the intervals of sea service or when superannuated.

The wording on their tablet reads

To the Glory of God and in memory of their Brethren of bygone days who for a long period carried on at the Port of Leigh the work of their Guild, this tablet has been placed by the Elder Brethren of the Corporation of Trinity House, London, in the year of Our Lord, 1906. Living in this parish they laboured worthily for the welfare of the mariners; and, dying, were laid to rest in this churchyard.

Some of them were distinguished in the service of their country and the names of those tombs or monuments that can be traced are here recorded. Their tombs and those of their kindred have been repaired and their epitaphs, with the exception of that on the tomb of Admiral Nicholas

Haddock, which has perished, have been transcribed into two books, one of which is deposited with the registers of the church and the other in the library of Trinity House, Tower Hill, London.

The Elder Brethren also desire to honour the faithful services of others, though their final resting places are not known, and to add their names if these should come to light.

Richard Haddock. Died 1453.

John Haddock. Son of the above.

Captain Richard Haddock. Died 1660. A Brother of Trinity House.

Captain William Haddock. Died 1667. Son of the above.

Sir Richard Haddock. Died 1714. Son of the above. Comptroller of H M Navy and Master of Trinity House, 1687.

Admiral Nicholas Haddock. Died 1746. Son of the above. Buried with 15 others in the churchyard of this church

Robert Salmon. Died 1471.

Thomas Salmon. Died 1576.

Robert Salmon. Died 1591. Master of Trinity House, 1588.

Robert Salmon. Died 1641. Master of Trinity House. 1617.

John Bundocke. Died 1601.

John Bundocke. Died 1652. Son of the above. A Brother of the Trinity House.

Richard Chester. Died 1632. Master of the Trinity House, 1615.

Captain William Goodlad. Died 1639. Chief Commander of the Greenland Fleet and Master of Trinity House, 1638.

Captain Richard Goodlad. Died 1693. A Brother of Trinity House.

James Moyer. Died 1661. A Brother of the Trinity House, 1630.

* * *

The Haddocks' tombs stand on the bend of the pathway by the east gate, where 15 members of the family are buried. A brass plate to John Haddock still remains on the floor of the north aisle near the Chapel of the Resurrection in the church, dated 1327. The fifteen illustrious Haddocks still rest beneath the turf at the bend of the east pathway. When their tomb was vandalised in 1989 it was re-sited behind the grave of my great-great-grandparents, John and Susan Little, where my mother, Chrissie Brush, née Meddle, was interred with her great-grandparents in January, 1982 - the first interment in St Clement's churchyard for a hundred years.

The Haddock tomb

DUNKIRK

On Sunday, 26 May, 1968, the closely linked and inter-married families of Leigh filled St Clement's Church, proud that, at long last, our men and boats had received Admiralty recognition, a plaque and flags being dedicated in the Chapel of the Resurrection.

From the pulpit the Rev John L Head gave a wonderfully moving address taking the congregation back to the dark days of 1940. He told of the crew of the *Renown*, Harry Noakes, a nice looking, quiet lad, who, with his sister Nora, had grown up in Wharf Cottage on Billet Wharf; their father, a widower and ex-Navy man was fondly known as 'Rat' Noakes; Leslie Osborne, a happy freckle-faced boy, shy, but with a permanent grin and eyes creased and brimming with laughter, known to all as 'Lukie', the son of May and George 'Donah' Osborne; and Frank Osborne, cousin to both. Frank's father, also Frank, had married Ada Noakes, Rat's sister; she died when Frankie was only 10 years old and Frank, senior, had married his wife's twin sister, Lillian. She was a wonderful step-mother to little Frankie, but, although they really loved each other, he never called her anything but 'Aunt Lil'. Frankie is remembered as a handsome boy, always immaculate, with well-groomed dark hair.

The British Expeditionary Force was trapped on the beaches of Dunkirk between the sea and the advancing German forces and was under constant fire. The six most seaworthy Leigh boats were commandeered - the *Renown*, owned by the Osborne brothers; the *Reliance*, owned by William 'Toodley' Meddle; the *Resolute*, of Cecil

Back row:
Ernie Osborne, ?,
Frankie Osborne.
Front: 'Lukie'
Osborne, Grace
Bailey, George
'Pie' Osborne, 1937

Frankie Osborne

Harry Noakes

Osborne and his brother Alf; the *Defender*, owned by the Harvey brothers; the *Endeavour*, owned by H Robinson; and Arthur J `Woffa' Dench's *Letitia*.

A little after 10 o'clock on Tuesday, 31 May, 1940, the six cockle boats sailed from Leigh. Passing Margate Pier they received orders to shape a course straight for Dunkirk. The swell in the Channel had been treacherous for the past week and then, as if in answer to a nation's prayers, the wind had diminished, land surf had died down that afternoon. At 7 p.m. the little Leigh convoy was attacked by some 40 German bombers; zigzagging skilfully they escaped the bombs and, moving independently, reached Dunkirk.

As the swell was too heavy for them to go into the beach they began to ferry troops off from the outer end of the Mole. Working with the Dutch schuit *Tilley*, which had escaped from Holland and was temporarily commissioned by the Royal Navy, they were swiftly filled. Continuing to ferry troops out to deeper draught ships they ventured ever deeper into the harbour time and time again and, as the receding tide lowered the boats in the water, so the troops had to jump further from the dock side, impressing the studs of their boots on the decking of the boats.

`Woffa' Dench, the *Letitia's* skipper recalled, "We began our journey home. Soon we saw another boat coming up behind us. It was the *Renown*. Frankie yelled that they had engine trouble. They made fast to our stern and we towed them, about 3½ fathoms of rope being the distance between us. That was 1.15 a.m. and, tired out, the engineer and seaman and signaller went to

IN TRIBUTE TO THE FISHERMEN OF LEIGH WHO WENT TO DUNKIRK 1st JUNE 1940 AND IN MEMORY OF THOSE WHO GAVE THEIR LIVES FRANK OSBORNE LESLIE OSBORNE HARRY NOAKES HAROLD GRAHAM PORTER GREATER LOVE HATH NO MAN THAN THIS THAT A MAN LAY DOWN HIS LIFE FOR HIS FRIENDS

'turn in' as our work seemed nearly done. We were congratulating ourselves when, at about 1.50, a terrible explosion took place. The *Renown* had hit a mine and a hail of wood splinters came down on our deck. In the pitch dark we could do nothing except pull in the tow rope, which was just as we had passed it to the *Renown* about three quarters of an hour before. But not a sign of the *Renown*. These were Leigh men who had lived quiet, respectable lives and had never done a bad turn to anyone. Better living boys you could never have wished to meet. They knew nothing of war, they went to save, not to fight. They had done their work and now suddenly on their way home there came annihilation. It was a small tragedy in the great disaster of those days of war, yet great in the hearts of Leigh people. We still wonder why their bravery should have been paid thus."

'Woffa' Dench

Tony Pitt-Stanley with a model of the *Reliance*

LEIGH METHODISM

In 1748 two or three Leigh boats were forced by a Channel storm to take refuge in Shoreham Harbour, Sussex. Having made fast they slept aboard for what was left of the night, to be awakened in the bright, sunny morning to what sounded like a choir of angels. Investigating further they found a large group of people on the harbour wall, obviously enjoying an open-air service.

The Leighmen joined them and, when the singing ceased, a fair man in black, standing on slightly higher ground, began to preach. He was, they were told, John Wesley. So eloquent was his sermon and yet so understandably simple that the fishermen were enthralled by his teaching: it was a complete contrast to the Anglo-Catholic preaching of Rector Hodge at St Clement's.

After the service the Leighmen begged John Wesley to visit the port and this he promised to do sometime later that year. The Leighmen returned home completely converted, singing Wesley's praises to all who would listen. One who did was Dr Cook, the Medical Officer of Leigh, and he wrote to Wesley offering accommodation in his house, Cook's Place, when he came to Leigh.

John Wesley duly arrived on Monday, 21 November, 1748. It had rained the night before, followed by a sharp frost, and Leigh people began to get anxious as dusk began to fall. So six of them, including my great-great-grandfather, John Little, went out in a coach towards Rayleigh to guide the preacher into Leigh, arriving back at about 4 o'clock.

Wesley preached to a very large gathering in Cook's Place that evening. This was the first of six visits, the last being 11

The cockle sheds and the gasworks, Leigh

October, 1756, and on 12 November, 1753, he wrote in his diary, "Here was once large port, but the sands have long since drifted in and reduced a once flourishing town to a small and ruinous village." This unfortuately was true!

In the years following meetings continued either at a member's house or in the open air on the Strand. It was not until 1811 that they were able to build their own chapel, facing the sea on the north side of the High Street at the western end.

When the Eastern Counties and Blackwall Companies built the railway, opened to Leigh on 1 July, 1855, an error in planning brought the track right through the middle of the village, demolishing everything in its path, including the Methodist Chapel. With nearly 30 years of their lease to run the Wesleyans fought back and, in 1859, the London, Tilbury & Southend Railway built them a new chapel west of Billet Lane by way of compensation.

On 30 December, 1860, the congregation made a payment of £200 to the railway company, who enfranchised the chapel and its land to the Wesleyans for all time; the deed was enrolled in Chancery on 16 March, 1861. By 1879 the building had become unsafe due to the heavy rail traffic passing, so a new and larger chapel was built on the same site; this, in turn, was succeeded by the present building in 1933.

Thus, an Act of God - a storm in the Channel - brought Methodism to Leigh and today it remains a vital part of Leigh's charm and character.

Members of the Society Class of Old Town Methodist Church, 1902.
Back row (l to r): Frank Bridge, Henry Johnson, Dick Deal, James Deal; *Middle row:* Albert Going, Tom Ritchie, Richard Harvey, William Kemp, Jape Cotgrove, William Bridge, Tom Robinson, Fred Partridge, Charlie Robinson, Jim Noakes, William Emery; *Front row:* Joe Deal, Bob Emery, John Brock, William Oliver, Elijah Risby, Richard Kirby, Daniel Lester, Robert Ford, Pilot Harvey.

SMUGGLING TALES

Smuggling was a time honoured tradition amongst Leighmen. My mother's grandmother, who was, before her marriage to William Meddle, Sarah Little, often recalled how, as a child, she was frequently roused from sleep by Coast Guards who insisted on searching even the beds when her brothers were seen to come in from a run. Nothing was ever found as the boys didn't store anything in the house, but at the top of their long garden they had dug a large hole wherein to store their contraband. They covered the hole with planks and a layer of turf. An uncle, known as Bibby, a dapper little man who used perfume and took snuff, had his arm shot off by the Coast Guards during a raid.

But the most famous of them all was Elizabeth Little, great-grandmother's great-aunt. She was listed in the *History Gazette of Essex* dated 1848 (the *Kelly's Directory* of the time) as a Draper of the High Street, Leigh. Her shop was where the Peter Boat car park is now. She sold the finest silks and lace, perfume and gin, all, of course, contraband.

She and her brothers owned a fast sailing boat and carried on quite a trade between the continent and the merchants in London. She was an educated, intellectual person and her dinner parties were something to be remembered, with brilliant conversation and gossip from abroad and from London, fine French wines and excellent food, prepared by her housekeeper, Madam le Gryse. Elizabeth was obviously the brains behind the smuggling operation and every inch a lady, but her love of excitement and the sea demanded that she took an active part in the cross-Channel runs. She could handle a boat as well as any man.

One particular trip must be recalled. Something had delayed their departure from Ostend and, when at last they reached the mouth of the Thames, the tide was against them and a Coast Guard cutter was lying in wait, letting go a shot across their bows. Elizabeth put on more sail and made a run for it. The cutter shot again, this time wounding Bob, the younger brother, in the arm. The Leigh boat turned and headed for Shoebury Point and then into Barling Creek, knowing the cutter could not follow in such shallow waters.

After half an hour Will, the elder brother, began to have doubts. "Liz," he said, "we've made a bad move here. When the tide goes out we're going to be stranded here like rats in a trap, with poor old Bob and all the stuff aboard." "No," said Elizabeth, "I'm going to take Bob and all the stuff overland and you can take the empty boat right out under their noses and bring her back to Leigh." Then she pointed her finger in a southwesterly direction and said to Will, "Do you see Little Wakering Church, Will? Close by there is an undertaker named Benniworth. Go over and tell him that I have need of a coffin and his hearse; I will pay him well." Half an hour later saw them on the road to Bournes Green with Bob safely installed in the coffin, the loot carefully packed on the floor and Elizabeth seated upfront wrapped in her black shawl as if in deep mourning.

Everything went according to plan and, later in the day when Bob had been attended to and hearse and horse were securely put away in the stable at the rear

The Peter Boat (burnt down 1892). On the right Elizabeth Little's shop. John Constable's white house opposite

37

of the house, Mr Benniworth and Elizabeth, relaxing over glasses of rare French brandy, greeted Will's safe return with peals of triumphant laughter. Benniworth proved to be a man with a great sense of humour, despite his calling.

The undertaker told them how he breathed a sigh of relief as he turned his horse over the brow of Leigh Hill. Then, suddenly, as they passed Bank House on his left, he saw to his horror that just ahead of them to his right, by the gateway to Eden Lodge, was a Customs Officer. Taking a step towards the road the Officer raised his hand to apprehend them - or so Mr Benniworth feared - but then, to his surprise, the official simply raised his hat and cast his eyes down in respect to Elizabeth. It was all Mr Benniworth could do to stop himself from laughing out loud. Indeed, when the tale was retold, all of Leigh laughed: this was a story that Leigh was to enjoy for many a year.

Late one January night in 1892 the landlord of the Peter Boat and his brother-in-law staggered together up the dark staircase, having partaken of a considerable amount of ale. One of them, who was carrying the lamp, stumbled and fell. A resounding crash echoed through the building, there was a blinding flash and the west wall and stairs began to blaze.

Both men, sobered by shock, rushed into the street shouting, "Fire! Fire!" and fishermen, roused from their sleep, came out of their houses to see the timber-framed Essex weatherboarded tavern burning furiously. The Leighmen rushed down Alley Dock, dammed up the Creek to trap the receding tide and formed a chain of men with buckets in an endeavour to stem the blaze, but to no avail, and this ancient tavern burnt to the ground. So too did all the timbered cottages to the east, as far as the Strand, some dating back to Tudor days with picturesque overhung upper storeys.

In the cold light of day the reason for the anxiety of the Leigh fishermen and their frantic efforts of the previous night was plainly revealed to all, for there - fully exposed - was the cellar beneath the beer cellar; the storehouse for Leigh's smuggled contraband, in which all were involved.

The fog lay in dense patches over the marshes and Hadleigh fields in January, 1829. The Leigh fishermen edged their punts along the creek between the sea wall and Two Tree Marsh silently with muffled oars. There were about ten boats in all, low in the water, weighed down with their cargo of contraband - rum and brandy.

Reaching the appointed spot where they were to rendezvous with the overland smugglers they shipped oars and made fast. Now they had to wait for their signal to unload from the lookout on Castle Hill. The wait seemed like an eternity to their tense nerves. One or two laid flat up against the sea wall, straining their eyes into the milky distance.

A dull thud alerted them just as the boats swung around with the changing current, warning them that the tide had turned. They should have been unloaded and well away by now for it would be daylight in less than an hour. Suddenly, on the flat ground between the lower Castle slopes and the sea wall a small figure was seen to break cover and run in a northwesterly direction. A shot rang out, echoing and re-echoing cross the bleak

Houses burnt down in the 1892 Peter Boat fire

marshland, and the running figure dropped like a stone.

"Gawd," said one of the Leighmen, "that's a warning. Them perishin' coast-guards are up there waiting on us... Let's get 'ome out on it."

"No," said a man on the wall. "That chap a-laying out there risked his life to warn us. He's still alive, I just see 'im a-moving towards us along the edge on that there ditch and I'm a-goin' over there ter git 'im." Cautiously and flat on his belly, he made the journey and returned with a badly wounded boy of about 14 years old.

Greatly helped by the fast ebbing tide, they made excellent time on the return journey and, before long, the ill-fated cargo and the wounded runner were safely

installed in the cellar below the beer cellar in the Peter Boat. A bed was brought for the boy, but despite careful nursing and daily visits by the doctor, by the end of the week he died.

It was obvious, of course, that if his death was reported in the customary way, awkward questions would inevitably be asked: "Where did he come from?"... "What were the circumstances of his death?"... "Who attended him?"... "Why did the doctor not report the shooting to the proper authorities?"... "Where did he die?" To reveal the existence of their secret storehouse would have meant an end to all future smuggling activity and prosecution for almost the entire village.

It was generally agreed that the boy

must be removed from the cellar and buried in a less incriminating spot, somewhere where he could not be connected with that disastrous run or the men he had saved. A place had to be found far enough removed to disassociate itself from them personally and yet somewhere in view of all of them, where they could observe without drawing attention to their interest. And so it was unanimously agreed that he should be buried on the marsh.

So on one moonless night during the third week in January this brave lad was laid to rest - and that should have been an end to the affair. But Fate took a hand. The usual high tides at that time of the year completely submerged the area in the first week in February and, as it retreated for the last time, it revealed its secret. It was the coastguard and the constable who brought the boy's body to the mortuary in the southeast corner of the churchyard.

It was Tom Green of Billet Cottage who entrusted me with this story, among so many others, when I was a child, and it was many years later when research among the registers of St Clement's Church gave me the corroboration I needed. The relevant passage reads:

Page 40

February 5th, 1829

[and in the space intended for the name of the deceased, the Rector had written in full]

A lad about the age of 13 or 14 found underneath earth in a bank on the Saltings, Leigh Marsh.

Buried by Coroner's Warrant. Place of residence unknown.

Signed E N Walter, Rector.

Edward Newton Walter was appointed Rector of St Clement's Church in 1808 and it was he who established two services on Sundays. He was considered a splendid reader and a good preacher.

His son, George, a retired Marine Officer, returned home to Leigh in December, 1828, and, observing the haphazard, half-hearted attempts of the local fishermen at smuggling, reorganised this vital activity. He planned each run like a military manoeuvre and under his leadership and supervision success followed success.

Influential people and local dignitaries were persuaded to turn a blind eye and enjoy the benefits, of a regular cask of brandy discreetly placed on their doorsteps by nameless benefactors. Even the Rector received his ration without question, while his parish had never enjoyed so much prosperity and good living. Gin became so plentiful and commonplace that Leigh housewives cleaned their windows with it - achieving a most brilliant sparkle!

Only one person became apprehensive - Mary Newton Walter, George's mother. She was a shrewd person and anxiously observed her son's regular coming and going, coinciding as it did with each run. She confronted him with her suspicions and begged him to abandon this dangerous way of life, but George saw no risk in what he was doing and continued his preparations for the following run.

He tried to convince her that conditions were really favourable that night - a night without a moon and the tide just right so that he would be able to be back before daylight the next day, bringing her a fine

French lace shawl. In a desperate attempt to stop him, his mother grabbed his powder flask and flung it on the fire. There was a blinding flash and her extended right hand was completely shattered.

George was beside himself with grief and, at the earliest possible opportunity, took a ship to Belgium, returning a few weeks later with an artificial cork hand so cleverly contrived that his mother was soon able to use a spoon and fork. He also brought back, to the envy of many church ladies, one dozen pairs of Brussels lace mittens to camouflage his mother's deformity. Eventually she was even able to use a sewing needle.

As for George, he began to live a more conservative life in keeping with his position as a retired officer and the son of a Rector. Apart from investing in the railway company, he formed a local Annuity and Endowment Society. He later married, living in Scratton Terrace in Southend.

On 15 July, 1854, he saw the opening of the railway, bisecting Leigh village, and weeks later, on 24 August, he died. George had insisted on being brought back to Leigh to be buried among those he had known and loved, but, just as surely as the railway cut Leigh in two, so the shaft of his granite cross headstone now lies out there in the churchyard in two parts! His father had died in 1837, but he was not buried in Leigh, but in the churchyard of St Mary's, Lewisham.

THOMAS CONSTABLE'S MANSION HOUSE

John Constable's Mansion was one of the larger houses in Leigh and will be remembered by many Leighmen as Juniper's Cottage, although this was a misnomer. Built about 1589 the property passed a quiet life at the hands of various owners; by 1847 it was listed in the Tithe Awards and locally known as Thomas Constable's Mansion House, Thomas being the uncle of the artist, John Constable.

It is well known in the art world that the young John Constable travelled from East Bergholt, Suffolk, to stay with his uncle in Leigh at a time when his wife, Maria Bicknell, was ailing and it was considered that the sea air would be beneficial to her health. While they sojourned at the comfortable and roomy house, John Constable made sketches of the surrounding countryside, one of which was of Hadleigh Castle, later committed to canvas now hanging in the Tate Gallery.

His visit can be confirmed by a Leigh resident, Kathleen Hinton (née Ford), whose family was the last to occupy the house. She remembers quite clearly a pane of glass scratched with the following

Here I stand both day and night
To keep out cold and let in light.

It was signed by John Constable and a Mr Randolph. Who the latter was I have not discovered.

Recent history shows that just before the 1914-18 War the house was divided in two, one half being occupied by the Ford family, the other by a German Jewish refugee named Joe Juniper, who used the premises as a wet fish shop, having a smoke house at the rear and erecting a sign to this effect. Newcomers to Leigh used his name and, although he was a delightful gentleman, he has no more claim to the name of the premises than the Fords and, as they were already local people, it might have been more appropriate had the building been known as Ford's Cottage. The Fords used the shop as a teashop and café, and selling seafood from a stall at the front.

Sadly, Constable's House was demolished in 1952 - when it was found that it was pegged and grooved and, had it been left alone, it would have stood for at least another hundred years. The site today is occupied by Mike's Boatyard.

The Market Square with John Constable's Mansion House

ADAMS ELM

We can only speculate as to how many centuries Adam's Elm grew and dominated that part of Leigh to which it gave its name. It is known to have stood between what is now known as Station Road and Cranleigh Drive. Before the turn of the century, when these roads were still farm fields, it would have been described as Adam's Elm by Three Wantz Way. It was said to have been a magnificent tree, measuring about 30 feet in circumference and hollow, so that a dozen men could stand inside it. Many a keg of smuggled brandy was stored therein to await collection by overland 'Gentlemen'.

We know too that Adam's Elm Farm was sold in 1780 to William Webb for £800 and again in 1861 to Lawrence Davis. He farmed there until 29th September, 1880, when the land was sold for building and the farmhouse became the Elm Hotel.

In the 1920s when alterations to the building were in progress a nine page manuscript in a bottle was discovered in the rafters of the old farmhouse. It had been written by Lawrence Davis and told of the slavery of working during the agricultural depression, saying that he had not made a shilling profit in twenty years. So poverty-stricken were the farmers that Rector Walker King had returned the tithe money. The document also records that William Thorp carried out the joinery work on the farm, no doubt from the Leigh Hill carpenters and undertakers established in 1838. A copy of the manuscript was taken and the original resealed and returned to the rafters, where, presumably, it still remains.

In 1980 a misinformed new landlord decided to change the name to the Hadleigh Fourpenny, a name with no connection with the site and out of context that was unacceptable to Leigh people. About this time the old age pensioners' flats on the old Howard's Dairy site were planned and Leigh folk campaigned to claim the lost identity of the locality. On behalf of the Leigh Society, as its President, I suggested that the flats be known as Elm Court or Elm Lodge, but this was turned down by the Post Office, the Council finally accepting my alternative suggestion of Adam's Elm House instead. The new landlord of the hotel bowed to popular demand and quietly dropped the new name, reinstating the Elms.

A CLANDESTINE BIRTH

Elizabeth Thompson (née Little) was in labour in Leigh village. It was August, 1804, and the local midwife of the day was Mrs Joscelyne, a close friend of Elizabeth's. To help while away the long hours of labour she revealed the strange circumstances surrounding another baby she had recently delivered.

Mrs Joscelyne lived in Joscelyne Square, south of Eden Lodge and one night at about 2 or 3 o'clock in the early hours of the morning she was awakened by a bold rap on the door. When she opened it she saw a carriage waiting in the driveway and a coachman who urged her to accompany him at all possible speed. Once inside the carriage the blinds were drawn and she was sworn to secrecy. She was taken across rough country roads for what she estimated was about 45 minutes until the coach came to a halt outside a beautiful old country house in its own grounds, The Lawns', Southchurch.

She was further charged to keep the visit a closely guarded secret and she was taken upstairs to a large, sumptuously furnished bedchamber. There she saw a woman with a beautiful face and cascades of rich auburn hair in the advanced stages of labour. Although she was the most lovely woman Mrs Joscelyne had ever seen, when the bedcovers were drawn away, they revealed a very large body which did not owe its size entirely to pregnancy.

She delivered the woman of a sickly girl and, as she was preparing to leave, a man with the bearing of someone used to authority strode into the room. He was wearing a clerical grey suit in the fashion of the day; the sleeve was pinned up and one of his eyes was covered by a green eye patch. His fair hair was tied back in a queue. It is unlikely that she was supposed to have seen this gentleman and she was hastily rushed from the room, paid double her usual fee and brought home.

Once again she was told to keep her visit to herself, but in her own mind she knew that the father of the child was none other than Horatio, Lord Nelson, himself. It was her firm conviction that she had brought Lady Hamilton's second daughter, Emma, into the world. Sadly, the child died before the next spring. The great man sailed for Toulon on the *Medusa* shortly after the birth.

My research suggests that Nelson's movements during 1804 make it quite possible for him to have been there on the night of the birth. Emma Hamilton was at Southend from the end of that July and she stayed for a month or more. As for the Admiral, documented and authenticated evidence shows that on 5th July he was at Sheerness, 18th July at Boxhill with the Hamiltons, 27th July back at Sheerness, 2nd August he sailed for Harwich, 11th August back at Sheerness to receive the Freedom of the City, 12th August at Margate and on 17th August he was at Deal.

I have never felt that Mrs Joscelyne could have been blamed for telling her story - after all, had she not betrayed her confidence Leigh legends would have been the poorer!

The Lawns at Southchurch

THE SEA WITCH

Rochford Hundred is famous as being 'Witch Country', but it was only just over a hundred years ago that Leigh was dominated by a 'Sea Witch'. Her name was Sarah Moore and in 1867 she lived in a tiny cottage off Victoria Wharf. She was a dirty, unwashed, toothless creature with a hard, weatherbeaten face, a hooked nose and a hare lip. Moreover, she was quick to take offence if she detected any hint of derision in a passer by.

Bizarre though it may seem, her own disfigured mouth appeared more than once on faces of new born children whose mothers, innocently or otherwise, had offended Mother Moore. Her curses were permanent and far-reaching to descendants even to the third and fourth generation. It can be seen, it is said, in some Leigh families today.

As far as my own family is concerned this curse originated from an incident in the family's history. It was late in January, 1850, and my great-great-grandmother, Eliza Meddle, expecting her third baby, walked slowly homeward with her two children, Stephen (aged 5) and Mary-Anne (aged 3½), when suddenly they were confronted by the Sea Witch with outstretched palm offering to foretell the sex of the unborn child Eliza was carrying.

Being a practical, outspoken person, Eliza, in the emphatic manner of a Leigh-woman, said, "I wouldn't like. I've got better things to do with my money than give it to you for gin."

"Oh, yes, I sh'ink you have, my fine lady," snarled Mother Moore. "You're worried sick about having one more mouth to feed, ain't yer? But, mark my words, not one mouth, but two mouths... and my mouth it will be," she said, indicating her own twisted lips. She pushed her face right close up to Eliza, who caught her a sharp slap across the face.

The Witch recoiled with a hiss, "You'll be sorry for that, my fine lady! You and all the females that come after you. All on 'em'll know the worry and heartache of bringing up their children alone and have you to blame for it. It don't pay to offend Mother Moore!"

And when, on 25 April, Eliza was brought to bed the Witch's curse was fulfilled. Twins were born, Elizabeth and William (my great-grandfather), born with the mark of the Sea Witch, the hare lip.

The last part of her curse continues into our time. Starting from 1877, when my great-grandmother, Sarah Meddle's husband, William 'Quiddie' Meddle died in a local smallpox epidemic, her son, William 'Toodley', was only two years old. In 1935 my father, Horace Brush, left my mother when I was almost 13. 1947 my first husband returned to Canada, leaving me to bring up our son, Johnny, alone. I remarried when I was thirty and had two more sons, Tony and Ralph, and in 1961 their father was electrocuted in the bath. I had to bring up three sons alone. I pray that the curse ends here. Surely we have all paid in full for that slap my great-great-grandmother gave the Sea Witch!

There are many more strange stories told about Sarah Moore. We are told that she had her own way of reading the future; she did not read the tarot or gaze into a crystal ball, she used an ordinary scatter bowl, a shallow galvanised pan with a

Sarah Meddle

'Quiddie' Meddle

'Toodley' Meddle

Chrissie Brush

wooden handle, as used by the fishermen. She filled her pan with seawater and carefully, sparingly and deliberately, she sprinkled in fine, dried, silver Thames sand from the Ray Gut. As it trickled through her horny fingers, rippling and clouding the water, she saw her visions.

She used quite a different method to foretell the sex of an unborn child, however, alternating the sex, month by month, from the date of the mother's birth. In the case of a second child she counted from the date and sex of the first child.

Widow Moore

Never was she proved wrong and, even in our own times, my own mother employed the same methods and was equally successful in her predictions.

Even the Sea Witch's presence on the waterside would cause consternation among the superstitious fishermen. The fear that this old woman inspired led to all kinds of fantastic tales being told about her, probably the best of which is the legend of the great storm in the Thames Estuary that took place in 1870, the year of her death.

One day a new skipper, obviously unaware of the dangerous consequences of offending Mother Moore, passed her on the quayside. As he did so, she shouted out, "Buy a fair wind," as was her custom, but, instead of throwing her a coin, as others did, he merely laughed and boarded his boat. The smack had only been out a short while when the sky suddenly clouded over, a calm stilled the waves and the wind dropped. The sails became listless, as if a dark hand had been laid across the waters, and even the skipper began to get apprehensive. One of the crew began to cry out wildly, "It's the witch, it's the witch!".

Almost as he spoke the storm broke and the sky became streaked with lightning, thunder echoing all down the estuary. Caught by the sudden squall the boat keeled over on her side. It was then that the skipper showed initiative, which seemed to be an attack of madness. Picking up an axe he began to hack at the tangled rigging, which threatened to drag them all under water. "I'll kill that perishin' witch," he cried, striking the rigging three times with his axe.

At the third stroke, the storm ceased as quickly as it had begun, the sun came out and a slight breeze sprang up. In utter silence the crew turned for home. As they drew close to Leigh they saw a figure slumped on the side of the quay and discovered, to their horror, that it was the body of old Mother Moore, red with the blood from three great gashes in her head... killed by a mightier magic than her own.

This is the story Leigh folk have passed down from father to son. As a child I was fascinated by the legend, but as I grew

older I became more sceptical about her death and the telepathic killing. Significantly, the church records show that she had been dead some three years before 1870; it says, "Sarah Moore, died December 14th, 1867, age 80 years".

I have heard other stories about her, equally incredible, but research in the archives at St Clement's has proved that they are founded on fact. For instance, the records state clearly that in 1849 there was an epidemic of cholera. The marginal notes by that efficient and obviously tidy minded Rector, the Reverend R Eden, who himself nursed the sick, show that fifteen people were victims of this dreadful disease. Among them it is stated

Chollera. George Moore died August 12th, 1849 and further down the page

Chollera. John Moore, died August 16th, 1849

Both were sons of Widow Moore. Whatever else might be said of her she loved her sons as deeply as any mother would. The misery and the loneliness of the year that followed left their mark, with trails of bitterness, hatred and cruel victimisation of all who crossed her path.

When the almanack showed that a full year had passed and 12 and 16 August, 1850, was upon her she took refuge in gin. For two weeks she worked herself into a drunken frenzy and then she lit her copper and boiled up a most satanic brew. Mourning the fact that she would never now have grandchildren she cursed mothers with babies conceived while her sons still lived that had been born since they were taken from her. Filling her pan with this scalding evil-smelling concoction she went to the homes of five families known to her with babies of under six months and, on their clean white hearth-stoned doorsteps, she poured a little of her witch's brew, muttering her foul curses and demanding to know why their bairns were alive, while hers were up there in the churchyard. Between the first and third week from that terrible night all five were dead.

Although this sounds much too horrible and macabre to be true, again the register tells a sad tale. Here is the extract, stating indisputable facts - Richard Going. September 4th. Age 5 months. Mark Osborne. September 13th. Age 6 months. Gertrude Le Grys. September 17th. Age 2 months. Elizabeth Lucking. September 24th. Age infant
John Thomas Axcel. September 24th. Age 6 weeks

We are also told she had power to flash sparks from her eyes and kill people with fire. One Leigh woman, Jane Lungly, claimed to have actually seen this happen to her sister and her husband's sister. Her husband, Leigh's town crier, never actually agreed nor, indeed, dared to disagree with her, but one thing is certain. Both died tragically on the same day!

I have checked all existing registers and records and two of them confirm that this actually happened in the February of 1852 and one register clearly states that they were burned to death. On this fatal day, we are told, Lizzie Hays was minding the youngsters while her mother and Mrs Lungly were working at their 'lavnets'; she too would have been similarly employed

Victoria Wharf. Behind the pump is the Widow Moore's house. The children are Chrissie and Daisy Meddle

had it not been for her poor hands; warts and chilblains made her work painful and slow. She was going on eighteen, though quite small for her age and, perhaps, a little retarded. Janie, her sister, was around ten, Tommy Lungly was almost twelve and baby Em was just four.

It was a blustery day and they were playing in a sheltered corner of an alley on Victoria Wharf when a door opposite opened and Mother Moore emerged. She glared at the children as she passed. "Clear out on it," she hissed. "Play round yer own yard." Before the children could move she was out of sight. It was the banging of the door that drew the children's attention to the fact that Mother Moore had not secured her latch and her door was blowing back and forth in the wind.

Cautiously they approached and stood in horrified fascination as if at the very door of hell. On the far side of this squalid room came the glow from the copper that bubbled in an eerie and sinister way. In the middle of the room stood an unscrubbed deal table bearing a half-finished meal and a candlestick. On the wooden, match-boarded partition wall that enclosed the stairs at the far end of the room was the lampshelf, as well as the lamp. The shelf was filled with a couple of dozen dirty, dusty bottles.

"I wonder wot she's a-brewin' in the copper," said Tommy, "let's go in and have a look."

"No, we daresn't," replied Lizzie.

"Come on," urged Janie Hays. "Look at all them bottles up there. One of 'em might be a cure for warts and chilblains, Lizzie."

Once inside, Tommy closed the door

behind them, but they could scarcely see across the room, the only light coming from the one dirty, half-boarded window. Lizzie lit the candle from the fire to inspect the bottles more closely. Tommy and Janie lifted the lid of the copper, while Lizzie, with little Em close by her side, raised the candle towards the shelf. At that moment from outside came the shuffle of feet and a hand clicked the latch. All four fled in terror to the farthest point of the room, colliding with a bump against the partition. The bottle above shook and clattered over, spilling the greasy contents of one all over Lizzie and Em, who were immediately below. The baby cried out and Lizzie clasped her in her arms, Em clutched desperately, tipping the candle towards her wet dress.

The door burst open with a rush of wind and there stood the angry Sea Witch with curses on her twisted lips. At the same instant both the girl and the baby burst into flames. The children screamed and rushed to the door, Mother Moore grabbed an old sack and ran towards them, but they were more afraid of her than the fire and they dashed through the door and down the alley towards the creek. Their screams brought parents and neighbours out from their houses to witness this nightmare scene. The strong wind fed the flames until the screams subsided, leaving only the sobbing of Tommy and Janie and the seagulls crying above.

The doctor, the constable and Mr Thorp, the undertaker, were sent for and when they were questioned by the doctor and constable Janie lifted her tear-stained face and pointed an accusing finger to the back of the crowd. "She did it!" she screamed. "The Sea Witch. She came in the door and sparks flashed from her eyes and they burst into flames. She did it! I saw her do it. They burst into flames."

People turned around in anger, but the Sea Witch had gone to earth.

Tommy's explanations, however, between sobs, were more rational. He shook his head sadly and, with tears streaming down his cheeks, said in a quiet voice, "That stuff what fell off the shelf, must-abin paraffin. Some splashed on me sleeve, yer can still smell it. Em got scared when it fell on 'er and gittin' in Lizzie's arms she knocked the candle agin 'er and when the Witch came in the wind made it blaze."

"No, no," protested Janie. "It was the sparks from her eyes; I sin it."

"There, there," consoled the doctor, "perhaps you saw the reflection of the flames in her eyes; it was dark and it all happened so quickly, didn't it?"

"No. I was there. I sin it. She did, she did," sobbed the grief-stricken child. "An' she tried to catch 'em with a sack."

"Yes, she did," agreed Tommy. "She rushed at 'em wiv 'er sack an' she tried to ketch 'em."

There were many Leigh folk who chose to believe Janie's story and handed it down to their children and grandchildren. It made a far better story to say that the Sea Witch had power to flash sparks from her eyes and kill people with fire. Janie, however, emphatically maintained her firm belief in what she had seen with her own eyes until the day she died.

This was the legend, told by Tom Green, a Leigh man of over 80 years old, while this is the irrefutable entry in Mr Thorp, the undertaker's, register:

Emily Lungly... died February 28th 1852. Age 4 years. Burnt to death... Cost 10/-

John Hays' child... died February 28th 1852. Age 17 years, 9 months. Burnt... Cost 10/-

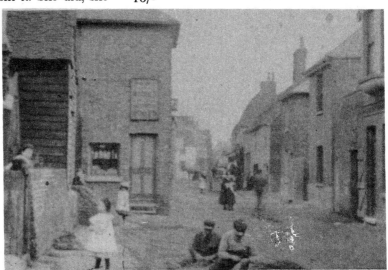

The Conduit

ALLEY DOCK

On the north west corner of The Strand is a shop, in recent years Lal Ford's sea-moss shop. In earlier years Jack Bray's `Snobshop' was next door.

The back of this was occupied by Ponto Boyton, who lived there with his wife and her sister, both of whom enjoyed his favours and bore his children. Ponto was the Champion of walking the greasy pole at the Regatta.

At the rear is Leigh's oldest existing working wharf. At the entrance to Alley Dock stands the Old Stables that, up until the 1930s and early 1940s, was used for the cart-horses that hauled the timber and ballast up the hill. It was China Cotgrove who told me that it was originally built for the smugglers' pack ponies.

Looking up the cobble-stoned Alley Dock to the Peter Boat, with its secret store room below the cellar of the old inn, one can easily imagine the line of pack ponies, loaded with barrels of contraband brandy ready to commence their overland journey up the hill towards Dawes Heath!

Alley Dock

53

The level crossing at the bottom of Workhouse Lane. 'Barrel' Johnson at his shop door

54

The Post Office, Leigh urban District Council Offices and the Fire Station

THE COMING OF THE RAILWAY

In 1853 the proposed extension to the London & Tilbury Railway through Leigh was received with growing anxiety as Leighmen anticipated that the line would by-pass the Old Town, rising up West Hill, over what is now Marine Parade, over Tiklefield, Duckmead and One Acre Field, terminating at what is now the Salvation Army Citadel at the junction of Glendale Gardens and Elm Road. Their town centre was planned south of this point to Rectory Grove, where, in later years, they built the new Urban District Council Offices and Fire Station (now the Police Station and yet another car park). Elm Road, then a tree-lined lane with a stream, wound away to the east and then north to the London

Road at Elm Farm. Here at the bend, opposite Glendale Gardens, they built their Town Hall (later converted into the Peculiar People's Chapel) and for the benefit of Eastwood and Hadleigh travellers a straight road was cut through called Station Road, as it remains today, with no connection to any railway station.

However, in 1854 the railway company decided that there was a more economical route - right through the heart of the Old Town, cutting off houses from their gardens, right through the Market Square demolishing all that stood in its path.

The Smack, which stood partially on the proposed track, near the Ship, was completely demolished and later rebuilt where it now stands at the water's edge, next to what was Constable's House.

The Bell, which had stood since Tudor times south of the present Bell Hotel, was completely flattened and the rubble from its building was used to enlarge King's Strand, thenceafter known as Bell Wharf.

The old King's Head, on the eastern end of the Market Square, standing defiantly in the path of the oncoming track, was cut in two and shored up on both sides of the line, with the trains running through!

Had the line gone around the Old Town it could have been preserved, along with many fine old houses that stood on the north side of the street and New Road, still known by locals as the Back Road. One modern author described the coming of the railway as 'cutting a breath of fresh air through Leigh', but in the opinion of Leighmen it was the beginning of the end of our once flourishing seaport town.

Will Foster, the owner of the King's Head, having been deprived of so much of his living accommodating the relentless advance of the iron road, bought land in New Road, east of Billet Lane and the Billet and west of the Red Hill. He built Pittington House, a fine dwelling with a canopy doorway and a terrace facing south. Here, on this terrace, one summer evening when I was eleven, I sat with my grandfather, Toodley Meddle, and his life-long friend, Frank Foster - son of William. I remember that on that evening I enjoyed my first taste of soda water in milk: the men drank cider. From the street immediately below us, over the line, came

Southend train leaving Leigh Station, c.1885.

Leigh Station 1896

The stepped entrance to the 1885 station buildings

the wonderful aroma from Tom Shaw's bakehouse, while the cocklers with their `grub-baskets' ambled casually towards the Mushers (the cocklesheds), past the Billet and the gasworks.

"My father," said Frank Foster proudly, "was the largest shareholder in the Gas Works and this was the first house piped for gas lighting."

"Yes," agreed my grandfather, "an' the night they first lit up half of Leigh stood down there by the gate to watch 'em go on. Half on 'em thought is was ago'inter blow up."

Now, as I recall that tranquil evening in 1933, Pittington House has given way to New Court and the Gasworks to the atrocious flyover bridge!

William Foster, formerly of the King's Head

Pittington House

THE WITCHES OF DOOM POND

The very mention of "Doom Pond" struck fear into the hearts of Leigh folk, for here it was said: "In the long-distant past witches were swum". Having been suspected of witchcraft, the unfortunate woman would be dragged, protesting her innocence, through the fields to the edge of Doom Pond. There, suspended by a rope tied around her waist, she would be cast into the waters, amid the jeers of onlookers. If she floated, it proved she was a witch; if she drowned, it proved the poor soul's innocence. One can only speculate how many families would wrongfully accuse their old ones of the Black Arts as a means of getting rid of them, once they had out-lived their usefulness - and there was no room for them as their young families increased. It is hard for us to imagine the terror and misery that these poor creatures must have experienced as they submerged beneath the murky waters of Doom Pond.

During the safe hours of daylight, Doom Pond was used for rubbish disposal, old beds and household waste. and here too they drowned all the unwanted litters of cats and dogs and it was a last resort for suicides. On Boxing Day, 1900, the owner of the Grand Hotel sent his son-in-law there with four barrels of rubbish in a tumbrel cart. On the edge of the bank the horse, possible startled, slipped. The son-in-law, horse, cart and the heavy barrels sank into the Pond and were never seen again.

From Thorpe Undertakers' ledgers now in my possession there are these entries confirming this:

To the Overseers of Leigh, July 24th, 1885,

Coffin for a man unknown. found drowned in `Doom Pond"

Coffin	£1. 0s. 0d.
4 Bearers	4s. 0d.
Attendance	5s. 0d.
Bell	1s. 0d.
Cemetery fees	7s. 6d.
Horse and hearse	5s. 0d.
Total	£2. 2s. 6d.

On Dec. 25th, 1903, Francis Eaby, age 65, found drowned in Doom Pond

Elm Coffin	£3.10s. 0d.
Single glass hearse and two coaches	£2.14s. 0d.
Four men and attendance	£1. 7s. 0d.
Cemetery fees	£1.11s. 6d.
Clergy and sexton	6s. 0d.
Total	£9. 8s. 6d.

My grandfather, John Brush, a master builder and carpenter, son of a Surrey brickmaker, was now the owner of Leigh

John and Elizabeth Brush

Park Brickfield, where part of Belfairs High School now stands, was approached by 'Scoppy' Bridge to infill Doom Pond and build houses and stables. He embarked upon this venture with doubt and reservation. Neither he, nor any other man, would actually want to live on the God forsaken spot.

He and his car-men began the daily journeys from his brickfield to Doom Pond with cart-loads of brick rubble. Time and time again my grandfather warned Mr Bridge that this hoggin would never hold secure footings. Still the dumping continued, my grandmother sometimes becoming anxious when these journeys went on after dark, as she remembered the story of the Grand Hotel owner's son-in-law.

My grandfather could not understand Mr Bridge's determination to complete this project and he finally agreed with John Brush and other objectors and the houses were never built.

The Bridge family had always been respected in Leigh, 'Scoppy's' mother had earned the distinction be being called the bravest woman in Leigh when she walked the length of a whale's back... but that's another story...

I remember when I was a child Saturday afternoon pictures were the 'in thing" for our crowd, and when we came out from the Corona or the Empire cinemas we would run as fast as we could until we reached the safety of the lights of the Broadway shops. My grandfather

Doom Pond

'Toodley' had jokingly warned me, "Don't stay in the pictures after you've seen them round because no self-respecting Leighman goes past Doom Pond after dark. You might hear them witches screaming."

In recent years I sat at a Leigh Society committee meeting where we were debating proposed plans in Leigh, one of which was for this particular area. I pointed out that this land had never been considered suitable for development because of the incredible depth of the pond and the fact that it had been in-filled with brick rubble by my grandfather Brush from his brick field. He warned the owner that it would never hold secure footings. How right he was! One of our committee members - a surveyor - assured us that with modern pile-driving this would not present any problems, so the plans were passed and Wallis' supermarket was built. Within a few months the land subsided and the buildings cracked. The shop had to be demolished and the site is again a derelict vacant lot.

Doom Pond, the deepest hole in Essex, situated in the darkest lane, which we know as Leigh Road, still has the power to evoke unease in Leigh folk. Recently I was approached by a local resident, living close to the site of Doom Pond, who told me that in the upstairs back bedroom of his house his family had heard on many occasions the despairing cries a woman. It would seem that Doom Pond is still making its presence felt today...

'Toodley' Meddle's *Jane-Ellen* at the cockle sheds

THE HAUNTED CELLAR OF LEIGH HOUSE

This lovely house stood facing the western end of the Broadway (formerly called Hall Road) from the late 16th century until 1927 when Southend Councillors mercilessly decided to demolish it to construct Broadway West through the house and its beautiful garden. The position of the house is now marked by the pedestrian crossing and the south-eastern part of the garden is now part of the library gardens with our beautiful Cedar trees planted by John Loten who was the Customs Officer and occupied the house for 33 years from 1815. It was earlier mentioned in the will of one Stephen Bonner dated 11th March, 1644, as 'sometimes known as Black House.' Some time after that it was occupied till 1670 by Sir Anthony Deane, the great naval architect, a friend of Samuel Pepys and his sister, Mrs Mitchell, who often stayed there.

In later years the occupants had trouble with their servants who refused to enter the cellar alone. They insisted it was haunted! - although at the time there was no obvious reason for such a claim. But local gossips tell that a few years before a pretty young housemaid and the dapper young valet were 'walking out together' and appeared very much in love. Eventually the girl became pregnant and the young man could not - or would not - marry her. Twice she was found at Doom Pond trying to end it all to escape her disgrace and a few weeks later the gossips said she just 'up and went' and Leigh saw no more of her. The boy friend who appeared to be distraught with grief left the house just before dawn one morning and descended the hill with a small portmanteau and on Victoria Wharf persuaded the fishermen to give him passage. As the tides receded beyond the main channel he walked ashore over the Jenkin Sands to the Isle of Grain and he too was never seen or heard of again in Leigh.

In more recent years a new owner of the house decided to deepen the cellar to lay in a stock of port. And beneath the cellar stairs they uncovered the shallow grave of the young girl. The skeleton was removed and laid to rest in the churchyard - and Leigh House was haunted no more.

Unfortunately the spectre of the destruction of this beautiful old part of Leigh heritage is not as easily laid to rest.

Leigh House

LEIGH NICKNAMES

Leigh has always been populated by lusty fishermen and the principal families are still here today

Axell	Boyton	Bridge
Burder	Carey	Clarke
Cotgrove	Deal	Dench
Dolby	Eagleton	Eaton
Ford	Frost	Gillson
Harvey	Johnson	Kerry
King	Kirby	Levett
Lucking	Meddle	Noakes
Oliver	Osborne	Palmer
Partridge	Plumb	Record
Robinson	Thompson	Threadgold
Tomalin	Turnidge	Wilder

It was the custom for sons to be given the Christian name of their father or grandfather, causing confusion if there was more than one man with the same name in a household. For instance, in my own family, my grandfather, William Meddle, was named after his father, as was his elder son: all three William Meddles. So distinguishing nicknames were bestowed, to separate and identify.

Therefore my great-grandfather became known as `Quiddie' because he did not drink and saved his money; my grandfather got his nickname because his younger twin stepsisters, Lily and Ada, could not pronounce `William' and called him `Toodley' from Tylty, the home from which the Meddles had formerly come; and my uncle became `Bailey' from the song "Won't you come home, Bill Bailey?"

It is generally accepted that all genuine Leighmen have identifying family nicknames. When someone in Leigh tells you that they have a local surname, you automatically tactfully ask for proof identifying definition. For example, if they say `Cotgrove', one expects `Chaser' or `Grannie', etc., to confirm from which branch of Cotgroves they descend.

Over the years I have endeavoured to compile lists of nicknames and, in 1967, in that excellent book *Old Leigh* was included a small register of names which proved disappointing to genuine Leighmen whose family names were mis-spelled or omitted. Unfortunately the author, who had so efficiently researched historical details, had turned to non-Leighmen for help with his list: I know this for, in the early years of World War II, while on duty at the ARP Control Centre at the rear of Leigh Post Office, I was sent to deliver a message to the National Fire Service restroom in a shop opposite Leigh Police Station and there I saw Mr Bride and a few off-duty firemen advising him on their ideas of local nicknames. Fortunately I was in time to request the correct spelling of my grandfather's name!

Just before he died in the summer of 1987 Fred `Whooper' Johnson offered me his nicknames, which are included here, with additions of my own, as a tribute to him.

AXELL	Aunt Margaret	Specky
	Bottle Arse	Raggy
	Steakie	Noah
BOYTON	Ponto	
BRIDGE	Fiddler	Brubs
	Shettie	Scopie
	Griffins	Cronjie
BURDER	Bonker	
CAREY	Bobby Unchin	Chicken
	Jim Dick	

Leigh Oval Well Cricket Club, 1922
Front row (l to r): `Baa' Clarke, Billy Mead, Horace Brush
`Pip' Thompson, Billy Foster,
George Meddle. Middle `Frip'
Thompson, Tom Kirby, Jim Kirby,
`Ike' Kerry, `Fonsse' Theobald,
Oswald Brush, Fred `Wooper'
Johnson. Back: Willie Cotgrove,
`Shrub' Noakes, Wally Cotgrove

`Flashy' Emery

`Cakka' Noakes

`Channie' Johnson and his brother    `Edgie' Harvey

64

'Hungry' Deal, Mrs Osborne and 'Chudder'   'Pie' Osborne

'Snappy' Noakes

Yola and 'Ingie' Emery

CLARKE	Cloudy	
COTGROVE	Gummy	Janie
	Cock Arley	Old Swaddie
	Chaser	Tom Muggins
	Grongee	Lumpy
	Bill Cobbla	Jape
	Arthur Rusty	Grannie
	Tea Graft	Ted Bolt
	Judgement	Tate
	Archie	Skinny
	Snipey	China
DEAL	Rudle	Ponky
	Ketchup	Churchie
	Hungry	Dasha
DENCH	Woffa	Musha
	Clickham	Itta
DOLBY	Fluffer	Wonk Eye
	Gold King	
EAGLETON	Pearlie	Tunnic
	Prossa	
EATON	Toddie	
EMERY	Welsh Annie	Pottis
	Inggie	Argo
	Kruge	Flashie
FORD	Squeaker	Tabor
	Tinnie	Swilly
	Marrer	Titta
FROST	Drunkard	Shitta
	Blowie	Fottie
	Docka	Goggles
	Joe Boddie	Bill
	Boddie	Gonna
GILSON	Yolks	
HARRISON	Sara Beck	
HARVEY	Tim Bobbin	Nabo
	Jack Niecee	Pugg
	RunWild	Nunna
	Jackie `Babs'	Porky
	Edgie	
HILLS	Dolly Pots	

JOHNSON	Whooper	Doodle
	Sweedie	Dimple
	Channie	Roughie
	Fuggins	Old Hundred
	Spuee	Brownie
	Good Alf	Barrel
	Changie	Bob Trot
	Stutterie	Goodwill
KERRY	Darbo	Putt Dina
KING	Trill	
KIRBY	Roll	
LEVETT	Lighta	Little
	Kipper	Bedbug
LITTLE	Whistling Billie	Zip
LIVERMORE	Tomma	
LUCKING	Joe Beckett	
MEDDLE	Pickle	Peck Itty
	Herbie	Toodley
	Gugga	Wuner
	Bailie	Old Soop
	Waler	Ganett
	Corka	Locke
	Quiddy	Shirts
NOAKES	Cakka	Frannie
	Snappy	Pope Rat
	Puddnie	Shruss
	Watt-Watt	Doctor
	Hopper Percy Treadlight	
OLIVER	Steva Bite	
OSBORNE	Neb	Lukie
	Donah	Chudder
	Billa	Ninety
	Ratsie	Doache
	Squidger	Bulla Pie
	Dank	Snipes
PALMER	Peddle	
PARTRIDGE	Happy	
PLUMB	Ricer	
RECORD	Pickle	

ROBINSON	Stouty	Fashion	WALLER	Daisy	
	Spikesley	Chatt	WEBSTER	Hattie	
	Tom Bowling	Charley Lady	WILLDER	No Matches	Emma
SMITH	Do Me	Blacken		Doughie	Tinnie
STANLEY	Capers (Eddie)	Johnny Canuck		Bobba	Earrings
TAYLOR	Onions			Abe Gully	Gibe
THOMPSON	Golden	Pip	Frip		Gullie George	Sid Gullie
THREADGOLD	Sweeney			Gullie Fred	
TOMALIN	Tattle	Moulda			
TURNIDGE	Bonner	Bully			
	Francie	Harry Buck			
	Shimmie	Tom Buck			
	Polly Wiggy	Poll Toots			
	Scheema	Rekko			
	Whitehead	Filma			
	Straight	Piley			
	Lightweight				

George 'Piley' Turnidge

On Midd Hill, Nelson and Mr Young of the Post Office

I have given you the legends of Leigh that
I heard from Leighmen when I was a child.
I wrote them down in exercise books, urged
on and encouraged by my old school-
teacher, Miss D. M. Nicholls. I researched
all existing records and registers,
endeavouring to establish fact from fiction
and found most of them to be founded on
fact! I leave you all to draw your own
conclusions!

Sheila Pitt-Stanley

INDEX